萬聖節

Customs, Traditions and Landmarks |
Non-Fiction Series

Copyright © 2022 by Level Learning, INC. and Washington Yu Ying PCS™
Original and Edited Text Copyright © 2022 by Washington Yu Ying PCS™

All rights reserved. No part of this book in whole or part may be reproduced without written permission from the publisher.

Published by Level Learning, INC.

Content Contributors:
Washington Yu Ying PCS™
Level Learning - Ya-Ching Chang

Illustrations by: Josh Taira

Leveling classification based on Level Learning standard. For full description, visit www.levellearning.com

ISBN 978-1-64040-026-9
Traditional Chinese Edition

About Level Learning:

Level Learning provides a literacy focused curriculum specifically designed for K-12 Chinese as a Second Language classrooms. Our program offers 20 levels of specific and detailed objectives, leveled texts and passages, mastery-based online assessment, and analytics to enable data-driven instruction. Level Learning reading curriculum for both literature and informational text emphasize grammar and comprehension skills to help teachers develop confident and independent Chinese language readers. The non-fiction series of books are specifically designed to support our informational text course based on multiple national standards. To learn more about our entire offering, visit www.levellearning.com

About Washington Yu Ying PCS™:

Washington Yu Ying PCS is a Mandarin English dual language immersion International Baccalaureate (IB) World school. Yu Ying's mission is to inspire and prepare young people to create a better world by challenging them to reach their full potential in a nurturing Chinese/English educational environment. Yu Ying's comprehensive IB, dual immersion curriculum equips students with global competencies for success in the real world. As a leader in immersion education, Yu Ying is determined to advance Chinese language programs and global citizenry education by helping other schools create and strengthen their Chinese programs. For more information, email: products@washingtonyuying.org

			十月			
星期一	星期二	星期三	星期四	星期五	星期六	星期日
	1	2	3	4	5	6
7	8	9	10	11	12	13
14	15	16	17	18	19	20
21	22	23	24	25	26	27
28	29	30	31			

每年的十月三十一日是萬聖節。這一天，人們會穿上特別的衣服，裝扮成不同的樣子。

有人會裝扮成巫婆,黑漆漆的長袍,看起來特別嚇人!

有人會裝扮成吸血鬼，血淋淋的牙齒，看起來特別可怕！

有人會裝扮成大南瓜。圓滾滾的身體,看起來特別可愛!

在這一天,人們會在家門口放一個南瓜燈籠。人們也會把房子裝飾成鬼屋。

到了晚上，小朋友們會一起去鄰居家要糖果。

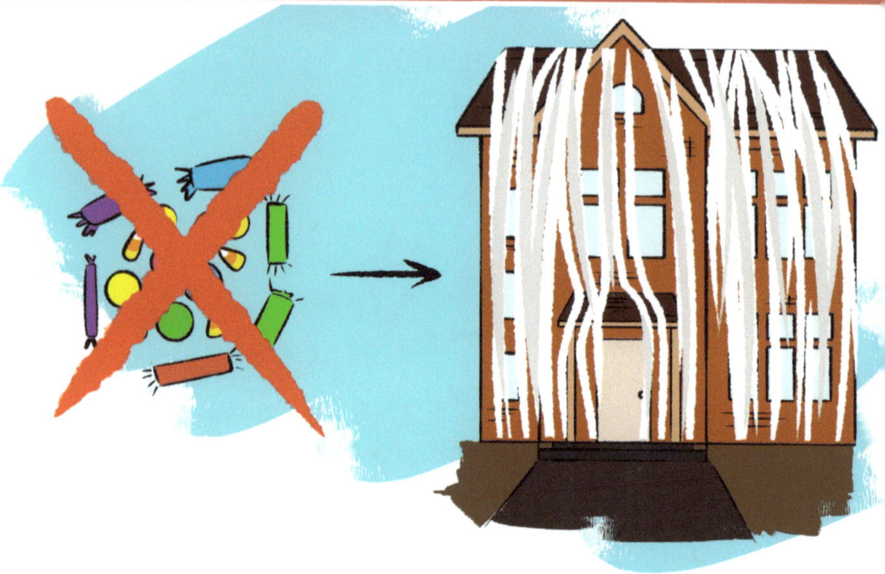

小朋友們要說：不給糖，就搗蛋！這天晚上，小朋友們都會拿到好多的糖果。

萬聖節真是一個特別的節日。

Glossary

	Pinyin	English Definition
萬聖節	wàn shèng jié	Halloween
裝扮	zhuāng bàn	to dress up
樣子	yàng zi	appearance, look like
巫婆	wū pó	witch
黑漆漆	hēi qī qī	black
長袍	cháng páo	long robe
嚇人	xià rén	to scare
吸血鬼	xī xuè guǐ	vampire
血淋淋	xiě lín lín	bloody
牙齒	yá chǐ	tooth
可怕	kě pà	scary
南瓜	nán guā	pumpkin
圓滾滾	yuán gǔn gǔn	round, plump
身體	shēn tǐ	body
可愛	kě ài	cute

	Pinyin	English Definition
燈籠	dēng long	lantern
裝飾	zhuāng shì	to decorate
鬼屋	guǐ wū	haunted house
鄰居	lín jū	neighbor
糖果	táng guǒ	candy
搗蛋	dǎo dàn	mischief
特別	tè bié	special

www.ingramcontent.com/pod-product-compliance
Lightning Source LLC
Chambersburg PA
CBHW041225070526
44584CB00001B/97